Little Puppy, Little Puppy, Noisy as Can Be!

By CHARLES GHIGNA

Illustrations by ELLEN STUBBINGS

Music by DREW TEMPERANTE

CANTATA LEARNING

WWW.CANTATALEARNING.COM

CANTATA LEARNING

Published by Cantata Learning
1710 Roe Crest Drive
North Mankato, MN 56003
www.cantatalearning.com

Copyright © 2017 Cantata Learning

All rights reserved. No part of this publication may be reproduced
in any form without written permission from the publisher.

A note to educators and librarians from the publisher: Cantata Learning has provided the following data to assist in book processing and suggested use of Cantata Learning product.

Publisher's Cataloging-in-Publication Data
Prepared by Librarian Consultant: Ann-Marie Begnaud
Library of Congress Control Number: 2016938052
    Little Puppy, Little Puppy, Noisy as Can Be!
    Series: Father Goose : Animal Rhymes
    By Charles Ghigna
    Illustrations by Ellen Stubbings
    Music by Drew Temperante
    Summary: Children interact with pets in this original rhyme set to music.
    ISBN: 978-1-63290-775-2 (library binding/CD)
Suggested Dewey and Subject Headings:
    Dewey: E 591.59
    LCSH Subject Headings: Animal sounds – Juvenile literature. | Pets – Juvenile literature. | Animal sounds – Songs and music – Texts. | Pets – Songs and music – Texts. | Animal sounds – Juvenile sound recordings. | Pets – Juvenile sound recordings.
    Sears Subject Headings: Animal sounds. | Pets. | School songbooks. | Children's songs. Popular music.
    BISAC Subject Headings: JUVENILE NONFICTION / Concepts / Sounds. | JUVENILE NONFICTION / Music / Songbooks. | JUVENILE NONFICTION / Animals / Pets.

Book design and art direction: Tim Palin Creative
Editorial direction: Flat Sole Studio
Music direction: Elizabeth Draper
Music written and produced by Drew Temperante

Printed in the United States of America in North Mankato, Minnesota.
122016   0339CGS17

TIPS TO SUPPORT LITERACY AT HOME

WHY READING AND SINGING WITH YOUR CHILD IS SO IMPORTANT

Daily reading with your child leads to increased academic achievement. Music and songs, specifically rhyming songs, are a fun and easy way to build early literacy and language development. Music skills correlate significantly with both phonological awareness and reading development. Singing helps build vocabulary and speech development. And reading and appreciating music together is a wonderful way to strengthen your relationship.

READ AND SING EVERY DAY!

TIPS FOR USING CANTATA LEARNING BOOKS AND SONGS DURING YOUR DAILY STORY TIME

1. As you sing and read, point out the different words on the page that rhyme. Suggest other words that rhyme.

2. Memorize simple rhymes such as Itsy Bitsy Spider and sing them together. This encourages comprehension skills and early literacy skills.

3. Use the questions in the back of each book to guide your singing and storytelling.

4. Read the included sheet music with your child while you listen to the song. How do the music notes correlate to the words of the song?

5. Sing along on the go and at home. Access music by scanning the QR code on each Cantata book, or by using the included CD. You can also stream or download the music for free to your computer, smartphone, or mobile device.

Devoting time to daily reading shows that you are available for your child. Together, you are building language, literacy, and listening skills.

Have fun reading and singing!

The children in this song have different kinds of pets. Some pets are big, and others are small. What sound does each pet make?

To find out, turn the page and sing along!

Little puppy, little puppy, noisy as can be!

I hear you.

Can you hear me?

Yes, I hear you barking, running through the park.

Just like me, it's fun to see you bark, bark, bark!

Little kitten, little kitten, noisy as can be!

I hear you.
Can you hear me?

Yes, I hear you **mewing**.
May I mew with you?

Just like me, it's fun to see you mew, mew, mew!

Little bunny, little bunny, noisy as can be!

I hear you.

Can you hear me?

Yes, I hear you hopping.
I never see you stop.

Just like me, it's fun to see you hop, hop, hop!

Little hamster, little hamster, noisy as can be!

I hear you.
Can you hear me?

Yes, I hear you **squealing** on your little wheel.

Just like me, it's fun to see you squeal, squeal, squeal!

Little parrot, little parrot, noisy as can be!

I hear you.

Can you hear me?

Yes, I hear you **chatter** when you start to talk.

Just like me, it's fun to see you squawk, squawk, squawk!

Little gecko, little gecko, noisy as can be!

I hear you.

Can you hear me?

Yes, I hear you **skittering**, pitter-patter, pitter.

Just like me, it's fun to see you skitter, skitter, skitter!

Little ferret, little ferret, noisy as can be!

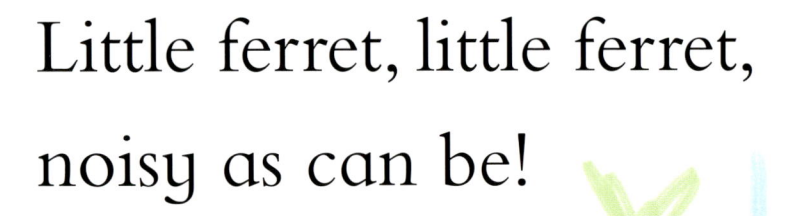

I hear you.

Can you hear me?

Yes, I hear you scurry up into a hamper.

Just like me, it's fun to see you **scamper**, scamper, scamper!

SONG LYRICS
Little Puppy, Little Puppy, Noisy as Can Be!

Little puppy, little puppy,
noisy as can be!
I hear you.
Can you hear me?

Yes, I hear you barking,
running through the park.
Just like me, it's fun to see
you bark, bark, bark!

Little kitten, little kitten,
noisy as can be!
I hear you.
Can you hear me?

Yes, I hear you mewing.
May I mew with you?
Just like me, it's fun to see
you mew, mew, mew!

Little bunny, little bunny,
noisy as can be!
I hear you.
Can you hear me?

Yes, I hear you hopping.
I never see you stop.
Just like me, it's fun to see
you hop, hop, hop!

Little hamster, little hamster,
noisy as can be!
I hear you.
Can you hear me?

Yes, I hear you squealing
on your little wheel.
Just like me, it's fun to see
you squeal, squeal, squeal!

Little parrot, little parrot,
noisy as can be!
I hear you.
Can you hear me?

Yes, I hear you chatter
when you start to talk.
Just like me, it's fun to see
you squawk, squawk, squawk!

Little gecko, little gecko,
noisy as can be!
I hear you.
Can you hear me?

Yes, I hear you skittering,
pitter-patter, pitter.
Just like me, it's fun to see
you skitter, skitter, skitter!

Little ferret, little ferret,
noisy as can be!
I hear you.
Can you hear me?

Yes, I hear you scurry
up into a hamper.
Just like me, it's fun to see
you scamper, scamper, scamper!

Little Puppy, Little Puppy, Noisy as Can Be!

Hip Hop
Drew Temperante

1. Little puppy, little puppy, noisy as can be! I hear you. Can you hear me? Yes, I hear you barking, running through the park. Just like me, it's fun to see you bark, bark, bark!

Verse 2
Little kitten, little kitten,
noisy as can be!
I hear you.
Can you hear me?

Yes, I hear you mewing.
May I mew with you?
Just like me, it's fun to see
you mew, mew, mew!

Verse 3
Little bunny, little bunny,
noisy as can be!
I hear you.
Can you hear me?

Yes, I hear you hopping.
I never see you stop.
Just like me, it's fun to see
you hop, hop, hop!

Verse 4
Little hamster, little hamster,
noisy as can be!
I hear you.
Can you hear me?

Yes, I hear you squealing
on your little wheel.
Just like me, it's fun to see
you squeal, squeal, squeal!

(Instrumental)

Verse 5
Little parrot, little parrot,
noisy as can be!
I hear you.
Can you hear me?

Yes, I hear you chatter
when you start to talk.
Just like me, it's fun to see
you squawk, squawk, squawk!

Verse 6
Little gecko, little gecko,
noisy as can be!
I hear you.
Can you hear me?

Yes, I hear you skittering,
pitter-patter, pitter.
Just like me, it's fun to see
you skitter, skitter, skitter!

Verse 7
Little ferret, little ferret,
noisy as can be!
I hear you.
Can you hear me?

Yes, I hear you scurry
up into a hamper.
Just like me, it's fun to see
you scamper, scamper, scamper!

GLOSSARY

chatter—to talk in a quick way

mewing—making a high-pitched crying sound

scamper—to run or move quickly and often playfully

skittering—moving quickly and lightly along a surface

squealing—making a long, high-pitched cry or noise

GUIDED READING ACTIVITIES

1. Do you have any pets? What types of pets do you have? What are their names? What sounds do they make?

2. Which is your favorite pet from this book? Draw a picture of it.

3. The pets in this song move in different ways. Can you scamper like a ferret? Can you hop like a rabbit? How does a cat move?

TO LEARN MORE

Hutmacher, Kimberly M. *I Want a Cat*. North Mankato, MN: Capstone, 2012.

Schuette, Sarah L. *Pets All Around: A Spot-It Challenge*. North Mankato, MN: Capstone, 2013.

Shores, Erika L. *Pet Dogs Up Close*. North Mankato, MN: Capstone, 2015.

Thomas, Isabel. *Beaky's Guide to Caring for Your Bird*. Chicago, IL: Heinemann Raintree, 2015.